NIGHT MOWING

CHARD deNIORD

UNIVERSITY OF
PITTSBURGH PRESS

Roy loved the hermit
Thrush.

6/1/08   Chard de Niord

The publication of this book is supported by a grant from
the Pennsylvania Council on the Arts

Published by the University of Pittsburgh Press, Pittsburgh, PA 15260

Copyright © 2005, Chard deNiord

Manufactured in the United States of America

Printed on acid-free paper

10 9 8 7 6 5 4 3 2 1

ISBN 0-8229-5894-5

NIGHT
MOWING

PITT POETRY SERIES
Ed Ochester, *Editor*

FOR

Liz, Soren, and Rayna

CONTENTS

vii

I think I could turn and live awhile with the animals . . .
        they are so placid and self-contained.
I stand and look at them sometimes half the day long.
    Walt Whitman

The new road o'er the forest is the right one
To see red hell and, further on, the white one.
    John Clare

I

RAIDING
THE BEES

RAIDING THE BEES

I went out to gather honey from the hives in the sourwood grove.
Put on my garment of honeybee clothes and packed the smoker full
    of burlap.
I thought of Samson on my way to the grove.
His hive inside the lion carcass.
His curse of hair and holy muscle.
I stared at the river when I arrived to steel my nerves.
Lit the rags until they burned, then closed the chimney.
I smoked the threshold bare with a steady cloud
that rose inside the storied chambers.
Cracked the seal of the super's dome and lifted frames
of honeycomb from out of the box.
How many cells filled to the top and sealed with wax for winter meals?
How many quarts of sourwood nectar distilled to gold?
I made a guess as they buzzed around.
No number sticks in the work of hunger.

TO HEAR AND HEAR

The hermit thrush is set for six
to sing his song, as if it were
the end of the world and he was stirred
by dusk to sing the same sweet song
again and again in the understory,
as if to say, it's neither words
nor meaning that matters in the end
but the quality of sound, as if we
were deafened by the sun and needed
his song as a key to unlock our ears,
to hear and hear and understand,
to see and see, knowing that this
one day is the end for now,
which it is, *it is,* he claims, with a song
just loud enough to pierce the woods
until the night descends like a thousand
veils, and then just one.

FROG

My tongue leapt out of my mouth
when I lied to her and hopped away
to the stream below the house.
Mute then, I started to write the truth.
My tongue turned wild in the stream,
for which I was glad and unashamed.
I listen now from my porch to the complex things
it says in the distance about my heart.
How hard it is to tell the truth inside my mouth.
How much it needs to sing in the dark.

SUGARING

You came down to me in the hollow after work.
I was reaping my just desert of overcommitting
myself this March to too many taps. I was resting
for a while on a stump, listening to the steady
drip of sap in the pails. You were dressed
in a skirt and purple blouse, whistling to find me.
I watched you descend through the trees like a goddess,
Diana's sister, perhaps, whoever she was, the one
who lost her modesty. I had ten more gallons to lug
up the hill. "You think each tree is a girl,"
you said. "The way they stream from their holes.
The way they yield themselves." "Yes and no,"
I said. "The way the first drop explodes
from the spout, followed by the second and third,
I thought of boys myself, but if you say girls . . ."
"It could be both," you said, "like Shiva."
I took you in my arms and held you like a tree,
slipped my hand beneath your skirt. I was happy
in my confusion about which was which with regard
to the trees, knowing then as I held you in my palm
and studied the trees that science is wrong
when left to itself. I was seeing with both my eyes
that the world was one behind the guise of leaves.
That the heart of my hand was deep with darkness.

THE METAPHYSICS
OF HUSBANDRY

The air filled my head.
A given for nothing.
I saw as I watched in order to see
those things inside the air
and hear them buzz.
So when I neared the compound hive
I stopped to see just what it was I saw,
although I tried in vain not to think.
Although my head was full of so much honey.
They were estranged from me
and ready to sting.

WHALES

For Heather McHugh

On a whale watch in Maine I saw
finbacks feeding on mackerel at the mouth
of Passamaquoddy Bay.
I imagined leviathans rising to the surface,
then disappearing beneath the waves
until they rose again for air
in a different hectare, spraying
the sea in geysers from out of the holes
in the backs of their heads, rolling
with the waves like waves themselves.
And then they rose at two o'clock,
three glassy backs the color of night and dorsal fin.
With such small eyes and powerful heads,
like scholars deep in their Atlantic stacks,
they must think without the means, I thought,
of getting down their thoughts,
except on water, written and erased
before the human reader can make it out.
I could feel their hearts as they ascended
and sucked the sky into their lungs
and arced again for another dive.
Did you see? Did you see?

THE BIRDS

I remember the birds on that forbidden day
when we went swimming in Paradise Pond.
A catbird whined at the top of an elm
and a bluebird called *hello, goodbye.*
A wood thrush yodeled inside a grove
and a hummingbird fanned the gladiolas.
A goshawk screeched inside the woods
where the sun cut through a hemlock stand.
A blue jay squawked on a maple branch
and a crow talked big in a yellow pine.
This was the day we wrote our names—
or they were written—across the silver mind.
So great was my blindness I saw straight through
to sky. I knew the names of all the birds.
Such was my knowing without even thinking.

KITTY

I called and called to no avail.
Each day was a ruse for the next, a subtle test
on which I thought I did so well, staying awake,
making calls, studying the psalms.

I added these sayings to my morning prayers,
"I am deceived by light. I think I see when I don't."
I took on the cat's inquisitive nature.
Got trapped in a closet and mewed at the dark.

Burned my traps on the altar of a mouse.
I fought to restrain myself from becoming extreme
and lost. Searched the raspberries for the corpse of kitty,
calling out her name in the criminal woods.

I called this day different from all the others
to the laughter of birds and squirrels.
Walked calmly through the briar patch with a box
of treats, shaking the vittles, scaring the snakes.

The past consumed me for a while.
Washed over my eyes like a cloud
with every scene of her life captured inside.
I came down with a fever, placed the cool cloth
of the world's disregard on my brow.

I confused my memory with her soul.
I saw her as she was and felt the sting
of this day's palm across my face.
Tasted the iron of night on the back of my tongue.

I called this day no different from any other
at sunset. The sky answered, "Everything you say
is turned to silence in the ears of animals."

I built a cenotaph in her likeness out of stone
and placed it in the garden among the catnip.
I wrote her epitaph on the base:
"My sweet ball of lightning. My little red coal."

YELLOW JACKETS

I was in awe of the way they lived in both
the ground and air, both digging and flying,
both demons and angels. I was ready to kill them
with gasoline when I noticed my neighbor's animal
eyes across the street. I could tell from the way
he was looking at the can that he wanted them dead
for no other reason than wanting them dead.
I put down the can and rose to the height
of the just-cut grass, high enough to see
the sills of heaven, yet not so high to keep
from burning with a few unnatural questions.
*Have you ever gotten down on your knees and listened
to the buzz of your own grief, then seen your face
in another face as different from yours as a yellow
jacket? Have you ever swelled with a tiny sting
then feared for your life?* I hit the ground with dangerous
force when he turned away, so high was that inch
to which I had risen. The bees awoke from the thud
of my weight and stormed from their hole in quick
pursuit. I fled like a fool into the street and then
his yard with a dozen stings on my legs and arms,
but oh what pleasure I took in causing him envy.

SHAMAN

All day the young obsidian crows
cried out in back beneath the pines
their coarse monotonous song, so urgent
and repetitious, so apparently plausible
to themselves, so intelligent
it wasn't funny. They have no teachers
per se, these masters of comedy,
these worldly martyrs. I took a drug
from the air to change myself. I forgot
every word I knew to speak their language.
I saw the earth from above, which was
a beginning. I felt the breeze beneath
my arms no longer arms, retracted my legs
like vestiges of human form. I felt
the deft excrescence of feathers
around my body like angel clothes,
and then what was left: an attitude
derived from hunger. A savvy look.
I imagined not imagining to keep this form.
I opened my mouth to speak on the edge
of town, in the crow-ridden suburbs,
a sudden bird in love with glitter,
a man without a mind who sang,
"I have become! I have become!"

A DAY IN THE LIFE

The Lord put a mark on Cain,
lest any who come upon him should kill him.
    Genesis 4:15

I put on my overalls and headed
out to the thorns with my blade, rolled
back my sleeve and swung the scythe
as high as I could to cut the thorns
at the ground. All morning I worked
in the brush, praying as I labored, laboring
as I prayed for a layer of skin to cover
the bone that protruded from my arm,
although it didn't bleed. I worked
until the darkness fell and I
could no longer see to swing the blade.
A pack of wolves surrounded me
and stared at my arm. I put down the scythe
and called to them, one by one,
until they came. With ears upraised
and eyes aglow, they listened to me
as I explained how the pain in my arm
had inspired the scythe, how the radius sings
and the ulna pines, how safe and dangerous
I am on the lam. The stars shone down
like all the bones that remain unburied.
When I finished talking, the wolves began
to howl and lick my arm, which soothed
my pain for a while and I slept till dawn,
dreaming of corn, waking to the stab
of rays in the wound the Lord had made.

CATCH

For Ethan Canin

I held the rod with both my hands
and reeled her in with steady drag.
I felt the force inside the line
like a current without the shock.

The surface was a rebus where
I saw myself at a certain slant,
then only dark where the mirror broke
beneath my face. A flash of trout

shone beneath, then disappeared
without a trace. It was that life
that I desired and therefore imagined,
a way to live inside the lake,

a way to fly and breathe the water,
a way to swim and turn like that.
Starving men report the powers
of desperate species granting wishes,

of talking mackerel teaching them
how hunger feeds itself, how nothing
lasts the way you think it will.
You do not want what you finally have.

I pulled her in and struck her head
with the paddle edge against the gunwale
until she twitched with only nerves,
then flipped around a few more times

before she lay outstretched and still
like the silver tongue of a god who lied.

I cut her open to find the hook
that she had swallowed, still coiled in worm,

then cleaned her guts in the lucid water.
I thought of things that I might want
but knew no wish was greater then
than the trout herself, caught and cut.

FIELD WORK

He laid her down on the lawn beneath
the elm and spoke to her in the voice
of God: "Good dog. Good dog."
                              I pinned
her down with both my arms.
                              Her heart
repeated fear against her chest.
The tumor had grown to the size of a grape
beneath her tail.
              He numbed her rear
with Novocain then cut the thing
from here to there.
                  The tumor fell
to the grass with a drop of blood.
"Good dog," he said again.
                          "Please
hand me the sutures and hemostat."
He sewed her up on the table of ground
to an audience of ants on their way
to the farm.
            The sky was cloudless
but powerfully charged.
                        "Good dog," I said
as one of the hosts in a quiet voice.
"Good dog."
            She stared at the grass
and raised her lip.
                    The whites of her eyes
eclipsed her look of usual trust, reminded
us of the bitch in her that's not a pet.

SIGHTING

There in the shadows another shadow at first
between the shade and dark at the edge of the woods,
just far enough in to flush the hermit
thrush deeper in, form enough
to rule a cloud or vulture out, form
enough to emanate the nimbus of
Humbaba's coat, form enough to make
me think that *he* exists inside the woods,
form enough to turn my head into
the woods, form enough to burn as form,
as Buddha said, form enough to purchase
weight against the earth, dent the ground
and crack some sticks, form enough to leave
the scent of a god in love: a bear with deep,
deliberate lumbering steps in just the time
it takes *to see* before she blurs into
the trees, and then the dark from which she came.

I saw the first cardinal this morning in the snow
outside my window at the feeder and was tempted
to call him my heart for his color, shape,
and hunger, but no, not yet; rather, little red bandit
at home in the north where the sky *conspires*
with the cold to form a blue so deep you can see
straight through, where somehow the voles dig deep
enough to survive the frost and the fox grows thin
but lives on bones till March, where the deer eat cones
and bears digest themselves in the dark, where all
things live, in fact, with the fear that they might die
tonight from the terrible cold and lack, although
they have no word for *it,* only the songs they sing
we call *the music of life.* I watched the cardinal
devour seeds by the dozens and then fly off, no less
diminished, to grow hungry again in a matter of minutes.
To remain on the feeder for a couple of seconds
as a ghost of the bird that shames the winter.

THE STING

A hornet flew up from the ground and stung my thigh
as I sat dumb on the mower circling the yard.
I turned the pain to thought as it swelled and throbbed.
I was blind to the nest in the way I was blind to the hornet
attacking me for what appeared to be
no reason at all, although there was. There was.
A selfless, perfect one, then more of the same
that followed the mower in a cloud of knowing. *Knowing*.
I regarded the sting as a sign of *the bee* that rises
from the ground at the thrum of the mower, or even my feet,
quiet as they are on the summer lawn, to sting
me hard on the neck or groin, then drag me down
into its hole, until I'm gone. I'm gone.

CAVE TEXT

I headed out against the wind with a spear,
wore a skin against my skin to hide my scent.
Already a few exhausted leaves fell burning to the ground.
A cloud lay dead on the swamp below the cave
and a raven screeched. I imagined a scene of buffalo
as I waited for the herd: the ghost of dust
beneath their feet, the blind low look of hungry eyes.
I believed that this attracted them, my need alone,
like the smell of grass in a distant field.
I took a coal from the fire that night and drew
my kill on the wall. I had honed a skill
for capturing their forms inside my cave.
It was the gift of terror that made them real.
I knew their lines in every detail,
their earthly beauty that was extreme.
I believed in the dark as a world in which
they would return on another plain,
in a different herd, but just the same.
I drew my figure next to theirs,
a winter tree with arm upraised.

THE OVERSTORY

A skin thickened around my heart
as the temperature dropped.
I notched a cherry in a thicket
of cherry for firewood, then cut its spine.
The tree fell clear as I stepped back
and watched it fall across the sky.
The first stars stared down like the eyes
of the dead and did not close or blink.
The darkness settled in the overstory.
I knew my blood was a drug itself
when I saw the sap ooze up from there.
The tree continued to fall inside my head
as I walked back to the barn across the field,
dripping oil on the narrow path the cows
had blazed, turning the earth into the world.

FROM THE BEGINNING ON

When we were eleven, Chris and I
imagined dinosaurs inside the woods
below the playground of the country school
that taught us nothing about ourselves.
What mysteries we didn't understand
we made up reasons for, the greater sense
that was easy to accept because we imagined
it that way, because nothing could have been stranger
than the way everything was already, especially girls.

Chris was the artist who knew before he started
just how and where to draw the first detail
that led to the others until the form emerged
as a dinosaur. We were on fire all day
with our subject, which wasn't girls
but the tragic life of dinosaurs.
It was as if we had to imagine the world
from the beginning on to prepare for girls,
to travel into the dark of an attic somewhere
where the first enormous creatures, long extinct,
resurrected inside our heads and bared their teeth.

We knew there would be no way in the end
to explain this to a girl who hadn't run with us
inside our woods, although we knew they thought
of similar beasts on similar trails that were worn
about the same. It was the terror of silence
when talking to a girl that caused us to acquire
such ancient knowledge about the world.

That taught us something godly about ourselves,
which was that every beast that passes

from this world grows in size and worth
like a pearl inside our heads, and that our heads,
unlike the mindless mollusk shells, can turn
them back to a grain again, or dinosaur,
in the time it takes to say her name.

THE FOX

We were walking together again
as in the beginning, listening to music
inside the woods, a medley of maple,
oak, and birch. We were talking
about something I can't recall
when suddenly a fox leapt out from the brush
and onto the road. We were naked then,
forgetful of *fox*, that way we had of talking with our eyes,
of fearing nothing, even in our sleep.
His eyeteeth gleamed as he turned on us,
the godly dog who wakes
from the siren of our falling asleep
to hunt us down in the same old dream.
We woke up then in different beds,
a pain in our loins where the teeth sank in.

II

SLEEPING
LESSONS

SLEEPING LESSONS

1

It is hard to remember when it began.
Someone said, "It's snowing!"
And so it was like a mother covering her child
already asleep.

A whispering steady fall,
it drowned the streets.
By evening she had closed her state.

It spread in the dark to every region,
smothering cars in fallow heaps.

By morning she had resigned
with lasting words for those in like distress:

"No vehicles allowed on any road.
Walk home and go to sleep.
Or if you are too far away,
lie down right there;
your home is where you sleep."

2

If my memory were any better,
my difficulty would be
the stillness of evening,
the subtle dark and spirit rising
above the trees;
no way for loved ones
to hold me down by the heels.
I am light enough as it is,
walking by forgetting, falling

from oversight.
Earth is the right place for love
if one can wake and still
have weight enough to fall.

3
They found a conch and took it to their room.
His mother said that it was perfect and smiled.
She told him to listen for its roar,
but nothing emerged.
"The sea will be calm tonight," she said in jest.
He wondered then for the first time about perfection.
The animal lay dead inside, like an ear gone deaf.
Their room began to stink,
and the ocean rose in foreboding swells.
"The animal is still inside!" the landlady cried.
"You must take it back."
They carried it back inside a bag
and laid it down on its corrugated side.
The hidden persistent teeth of ocean's edge
ground it into sand.

4
What I can't take back
is clearest in memory:
the look on your face
when I told you the truth,
the gum on my chain
from sawing the roots,
the chip on my blade
from striking a stone,
the glass on the sill
from throwing my boots,
the blood on the snow
from the deer I shot,

the love I gave you
without a thought.

5

"What kind of skull is it?" I asked.
"Probably a dog skull," Dad replied.
Mr. Evans agreed and asked to look at it.
I tried to picture the dog from the skull
but couldn't because of my memory of other dogs.
"What do you suppose happened to him?" I asked
without wondering where his body was.
"Probably killed," Dad said.
But I couldn't imagine him dead,
and so thought of him as still a dog somewhere
without his head.

6

A red Dodge Dart rounding
a rural curve above the James,
no guardrail, just the long, steep way
down to the tracks of the C&O.
It's my sister and her boyfriend
smiling in the front seat, her hair
flying as I lean out the back and stare
at the swarthy brawn of the current below,
thinking about how easy it would be
to disappear for good
into the hunger of its surface.

7

When darkness surrounds the house
on January nights, amplifying ice,
I turn to the most unfinished business
of the day and finish it quickly.
I think of tomorrow and see myself in it.

It is October again, Indian summer.
Leaves are falling on the uncut grass.
We are walking through the arboretum
reading the Latin names on every tree,
feeling the grades of oak, maple, and hickory
against our cheeks. We are achieving
obedience and faith, remembering the names
as a bonus of forgetting.
We are taking the true walk through
the arboretum, believing in intuition,
planting roses with each heretical step.

8

What was wrong with him to think
that he had been standing and waiting
when in fact he had been sitting all day?
The days were growing shorter for real.
He wanted to tell his wife that he thought
about death, but his tongue got stuck
when the thought occurred.
He wanted to kiss her on the lips
as she cut the grass.

9

Your peace below reminds me
that I have taken too long
thinking about what comes next.
Ribbons of morning fog rise
off the ridges and sporadic ponds.
Sweetness emanates as a bonus of beauty.
Apology seems pointless now amidst such splendor.
My fear was that the fish
would stop jumping if I woke you.

10

My father is in the hospital.

11

I am an addict with plows for feet.
Who will listen? Who will help?
I say the present is the future
when the prophet sleeps, much less the vendor.
Mushrooms wait in the shade
for the careless hand of a faithful cook.
I break the doors on entering and write in the cold.
My writing is jagged from the jolt of days.
A subtle wind drives us forth
at frightening speed, though slow at first.
My hand is this deliberate,
but once I wrote in a flash:
There is a hole for my neck at the edge of the world,
and a fiery blade that falls so fast
the mind lies dumb on the other side.

12

A breeze picks up during my walk
through the orchard.
Apples fall irregularly
to the rain-soaked ground.

13

This is serious at last, and I'm not afraid.
I will speak then with sturdy humor;
laugh and I will understand.
Trivia infects my heart.
The city park is filled with knocking,
flicker, downy, redhead?

14

I imagine others while holding you,
to have woman and stay faithful.
But I want to know the man
you hold. To see another who loves
you better, wishing I were he.

15

"Nothing's happening!" I repeat down the hallway,
"and I'm turning it as fast as I can."

16

I say I'm sorry now
when I bump a swimmer in the opposite lane,
and I no longer go out for gin
in the evenings; the lights seem stuck
and stopping is torture.
This is not a change for the better
but a result, a stage that will pass,
for I have dreamt the answers to waking up.
I will start running again,
and I will listen more carefully
to the opposite view.

17

This beauty of beach
spreads the deadliest germ.
I take it in like a suicide
but go on living.
In time, I will turn from quoting Scripture
to taking pictures of my little girls
in nautical dresses.
They are light-years yet from vanity.
The ocean breaks with hilarious news.
Not really but necessarily.

See how the earth buckles
beneath my clothes.

18
I am drying the glasses by hand,
wrapping each one in a dish towel
then opening them clean.
I am happy with this vanity,
holding each glass to the light,
remembering freely.
There is nothing I wouldn't redo.

19
The Adirondack chairs lay fractured on
the lawn, dismantled by a storm. Yester-
day I sat in one admiring the view
of sward and slope that rose in front
of me like heaven with flaws.
"Earth," I called it with confidence.
I am a weatherman at heart, a lover of clouds
in which I imagine and therefore remember perfect forms.
"What else if not the earth?" my love rejoined.
"The place that it suggests.
I know it doesn't exist and yet I believe it does."

20
Already she has passed the maple tree
where the forest begins.
She breathes with visible breath
and walks in a sacred manner.
Her eyes take off like birds and scan the earth.
She is accompanied by a cloud
and invites men in who want to go,
who do not see her for who she is,
who are left as skeletons covered with worms

when they emerge.
What diminishes to a point, then nothing,
grows also as large as Earth.
She offers a pipe and says, "Behold.
Nothing but good shall come from this."

21

There are times in the middle of nights
when I am falling toward Earth.
The weight on my back is not a parachute
but time fingering me down.
While still in the sky, I renew our vows
and watch the clouds rush in. I am dreaming of you.
I am falling experimentally.
The ground retreats according to my will.
Life on the ground suddenly clears from the blur of my hurry.
I am falling like a kind of telescope
through which I gaze without worry,
noticing the still existence
of things in their place.
I am falling.
A mockingbird sings on top of the chimney.
The pawpaw leaf
and army ant embodying the many.
The pawpaw leaf and army ant
bearing the antinomy.
Now you are there on the porch
in a cotton dress, your arms akimbo
and your head upraised.
You are waiting for me to land,
but I never do.

III

TIME
WAS

DUSK

I sat like a pilot in a grounded plane,
staring out the window at the slow
then fast descent of darkness.
I wondered, *In which form will it emerge tonight?*
Bear or fox? Owl or skunk?
The trees were shadows and the lawn was black.
I focused on a dove at the top of a maple
as the vanishing point.
Listened to the thrush's lament and thought,
What can I know? What can I know?
By the time night had fallen and the stars were out,
I knew that I must keep the grief of evening to myself,
that sadness searches for a body in vain.

NIGHT MOWING

Memory is a kind of accomplishment.
  William Carlos Williams

I remember the drone of Francis Temple's Farmall
mowing in the dark of a mid-September night,
its deep, desultory blasts were also guttural,
half motor, half cat, as it labored in the meadow
back and forth, felling hay in six-foot rows
with a sickle bar that rattled like a snake.
The memory of that mowing grows in my mind,
which is also a field that's overgrown
with every weed and type of grass, no less real
than the tractor itself mowing in the dark.
I wake with a start to the sound of that engine,
the same old Farmall I heard as a boy,
so that I am forever waking and remembering
at the same time to the accompaniment of a tractor
I cannot see in the meadow, but know is there,
as it is tonight, thirty years later, growing
newer instead of older as it takes me back
in its moving forward down the rows of waist-
high hay that fall like hair against the earth.

HAMMOCK

Finally the day arrived when a cloud passed by
and whispered *Enough Enough* as I lay
in my hammock, staring at the sky.
Halfway between sleep and waking I saw
that the voice of clouds throws itself into other clouds.
It was the last thought I had before falling asleep
beneath the canopy of maples.
It was dark when I awoke to the sound
of peepers singing their obsessive song:
It's time. It's time.
The stars were out like animal eyes.
A trail of clouds obscured the dragon's tail.
I imagined a hand at horizon's sill drawing them in
on weightless lines to hang again around the world.
I rose like a ghost from my hammock.
The entire world was singing to me
now that I no longer desired to write things down.
I sang a forgettable song without any words
that came to me like rain.

THE FIRST

A steady cloud of smoke rose from the chimney
and seasoned the air with maple and oak.
I was disappointed. I was glad. Another year
had passed like a week. I was tied to that day
like a horse to his post. I was angry at the way
it called attention to itself, *the first*.
Another winter day was all in southern Vermont.
I stoked the Vigilant with a thud and clink.
Let the silence speak from the empty chair.
Cinders fell inside the pipe. I drank some whiskey
straight, then walked outside to piss in the dark.
Burn this date on the vast white page of frozen earth.

MARGARET MILLER'S ARM

*In 1937, Louise Crane, Margaret Miller and Elizabeth [Bishop]
were in an automobile accident in France. Louise Crane was
driving. The car turned over and Margaret Miller's right arm
was severed below the elbow. Margaret was rushed to the hospi-
tal; Louise stayed with her. Elizabeth stayed behind at the scene.
She found the arm. She sat next to it and covered it with her
dress. She waited for the police, or at least some help to arrive.
She told me she had always wanted to write a poem spoken by
the arm, but couldn't.*
    Frank Bidart

Then I was moot, so suddenly strange
in the car, a clue at best to Margaret.

Elizabeth covered me with her dress
until the police got there and put me in a box.

I was naked without her, but no longer nude.
They buried me in a field across the road

without a stone—her empty sleeve my cenotaph.
It was an accident, nothing more, although it helps

to think there was for reason's sake—a sacrifice.
I'd take the blame for heart to save her soul,

as the Lord says an arm must do, but I was blessed
with strength and never hurt a soul.

I'm Deuteronomic now and will not bend.

THE FIELD

I imagined the field that stayed beyond the one
that gave itself to another growth—
the locusts first and then the pine—
was the one on which my memory depended.
I was sorry about the days I'd missed
by losing sight of the clouds I loved as a child,
by walking past the cows whose heads I'd held
against their will as a boy-on-the-verge of leaving the field.

I was sorry about the clouds that condemn
the slightest thing, as if to say there was hope
for me to raise my head, as if to say I had thought
too hard about what comes next. Time was
only the ash that fell from a stick.
Never mind the time that merely ticked.
There was time for me yet to make a change.

I walked across the field that was and that was it.
My body burned with each unfounded step.
There was a light beyond the light that drew me in
like a moth. This was the violence that bore away.
I lost my voice when I tried to speak.

THE PAIN THAT IS SO GREAT

Each day you watch the sun set
behind the jagged ridge of Bear Mountain—
day after day—until you've lost count, gazing
out your picture window at the western view,
distinguishing all the various shades of dark
for nothing until you wonder at the precise moment
of night just what it is exactly you're made of
that withstands the strobe of days,
just what it is inside you that resists the pain,
as if the pain itself were a part of you,
an organ the size of an orange or grapefruit
that can't be removed, that is as vital to you
as your brain or heart if you wish to go on living.

ANNIVERSARY

We sat at our table and studied the menu,
another eternal couple with an appetite.
Silence gripped our throats like a ghost.
I stared at the past as a single thing—
roses, roses, roses—and thought this
is what everything becomes in a moment
that burns to nothing, nothing, nothing.
What you were thinking I tried to guess,
and did, only to find how wrong I was, again.
It was as if we had fallen asleep in our seats
and were dreaming this. The sky was gray
and a chill had settled across the state.
It was, in fact, as days go, so forgettable
that we were privileged to remember it
as *the* day that took us back to the first
cerulean day when all we saw was *something*.
When dinner arrived on tepid plates
we raised our forks and began to eat.
Our meals were the day itself, June 20,
and we were tasting it, the blessed meat.

I was splitting wood in the maple bush
at the end of July when suddenly I sensed
a subtle change in atmosphere, a hint
of darkness inside the light, a bluer sky.
I put down my ax to notice it—what it was
exactly—a cosmic shift that marked the start
of summer's end, that put me in a vatic
mood for seeing ahead. I gazed straight up
to take it in. The clouds blew by as distant
smoke in search of a fire that hadn't yet burned.
The sky shone down as the high, clear mirror
on the back of tomorrow's door. The angels
applauded in the overstory, approving
the labor that never ends, that is the work
of *this* day, like all the others, yet close
enough to any of the six they still remember.

BOURBON STREET

The dead hear the music in their tombs and rise
to live again, if only for as long as the music plays.
How they crowd the marked off-street, peeling out,
getting down at The Famous Door.
The patrons think the ecstasy is theirs, sure as grief,
so selfless are the demons inside their bones.
So grateful to be both dead and alive.
Their faces are hardly wide enough to contain
their smiles as they move their borrowed legs and arms
to the blues guitar, the angel's voice, the devil's bass.

THROUGH A TRAIN WINDOW

There she was, my old girlfriend,
outside my window in a late-model
Mustang with her new boyfriend,
keeping right up. No farther away
than twenty yards. I waved at her
with both my hands from the other side
of the darkened glass. She laughed
at something and opened the window.
Suddenly, I remembered the sweep
of her hair across my face, how it
engulfed me in her with its lavender scent
and something else—a consanguinity—
with the force of earth I thought was heaven.
How similarly she had ridden in *my* car—
a vintage Chevy with a broken muffler—
to the way she was riding now,
over there, laughing at everything,
undoing her hair. I regarded
the boyfriend and wished him well
as he gripped the wheel with both
his hands, laughing at nothing, watching
the highway that curved away.

GATSBY PRESENTS HIS CASE TO THE
SPORT OF HEAVEN

I was naked on my raft in the late-afternoon sun
of August thirty-first, dreaming of Daisy in the pool
beside me, when suddenly I awoke to the truth
of how impossible it would have been to relive the past.
No sacrament of sucking inside my heart.
No whistling through the cracks.
No beacon on the dock.
I thought maybe in that moment that remained
following the shots that I could forget her at last.
That I could be myself again, whoever that was.
But no, I was lovesick to the end, ordained by loss:
myself as *me*, the Son of Man, come back to claim my love again,
although it was gone, although it lay behind me in the fields
that were resplendent, vast and lost.
If I have sinned in this, Great Sport,
whose fault can it be but yours?

DINNER WITH CHARLIE

I am moved like you, mad Tom, by a line of ants;
I behold their industry and they are giants.
  Derek Walcott

We're at the White Hotel.
I pick up my fork
straight out of hell
and pin down my steak.
Cut it with my knife.
"Father confessor . . .
Tongue all alone."
Charlie does the same
with his duck.

We feed each other
to practice for heaven.
"That's enough," says Charlie.
"There's only hell."
A red ant crawls across
the table as a sign.
We watch him climb the dune
of a napkin, traverse
the desert of tablecloth.

"High yellow of my heart,"
says Charlie, reciting Emile Roumer.
"I had to search for him
as a youth in New York.
This 'lowly' Haitian
who raised me up.
This solitary ant
on the table of America."

The hawkeyed waiter notices
the ant from across the room
and descends on him
with a silent butler.
"I apologize for this intrusion.
There must be a nest somewhere
that has escaped our exterminator."

"We were rooting for him,"
says Charlie, "to make it
this once, like Lawrence of Arabia."

A beautiful woman removes
her coat and enters the room
with an ugly man,
handsome from birth.

"You want dessert?" I ask.
"I can't decide between the crème brûlée
and chocolate mousse."

Charlie is silent for a moment,
staring into space
through the shadow in his glasses.
He's grieving the ant,
the beautiful woman,
and heart of the waiter.

"I'll have some more wine
is all," says Charlie.
"The cabernet sauvignon."
There is a draft in the hall
that blows through the room
and stirs the hem
of the beautiful woman.

"I'm trapped here by choice,
you know," says Charlie.
"Together we're trapped
in the country of poetry
that's almost as strange as America."

The ant returns
with a crumb on his shoulder
and bruise on his head.
We give him cover.
Charlie bounces in his chair
with a smile that's clipped
at the corners.
"We're on that ant," he says.
"He is our Atlas bearing us
into the world."

I GET UP WHEN I'M DEAD

The earth is more beautiful
to me now than when I was alive.
I am wise at last, laughing
at my grave, confusing my dates.
These clothes I wear were laundered
by the sky, pressed by earth.
I'm different now but still here,
smoking a cigarette that won't go out,
writing nothing down, finding everything
I lost but no longer need.
I'm never tired or hungry anymore,
although I continue to sleep in order to dream
and eat to taste the salt I craved.
Nothing has changed.
My heart has stopped, stilling my blood,
settling my thoughts.
I am still alive, slipping down
the street like the shadow of a cloud.

FIRST TOUCH

I remember touching Susan Bennett
on the inside of her left thigh in the surf
at Myrtle Beach by accident thirty years ago
and thinking it was a fish at first.
I raised my arms to the surface,
where they began to breathe,
then swim on their own out to sea,
followed by my legs and chest—
a school of happy, hungry fish.
I awakened then to the difference
between the groin of a girl and flank
of a fish. I said I was sorry as she swam
to shore, leaving my head in the surf,
where to this day it continues to bob
as a buoy, though Susan is gone,
and long since married.

FROM THE CURRICULUM OF
A GUILTY MAN

The furniture in the unused room grows heavier and heavier
Marriage is a bet with the devil
The fireman's duty redeems his prejudice
Judging others is permissible if you're writing from hell
An ounce is a ton in the underworld
The heart is a stone without the imagination
Death is spelled in every name
The dirt you shake from your shoes at the doors
where you're not welcome is enough to fill a garden
There is no other way to keep a secret than by telling it
Each night is an ocean in which you almost drown
The smell of pear blossoms is just as sweet
to the criminal as it is to the saint
If you think you're right, then think again

AN INCIDENT AT THE
CATHOLIC WORKER

Sitting in peace in the dining room
of the country community house one Sunday morning,
reading the paper about the latest truce
in Israel, I heard a disturbance in the living room.
People were scurrying and yelling, "Watch out,
he's got a knife!" and "Put her down!"
Then Kenny, the epileptic from Hudson Valley,
appeared at the door with a little dog in one hand
and a cleaver in the other. He said he was going
to take the dog up the hill and throw her in the well.
He said he was tired of how the people in the "community"
were treating him, and he had to kill the dog
in order to change their attitude. He had
a crazed look in his eye while the dog hung limp,
Mrs. Smith's terrier. I followed him up the hill
while the others prayed below. I said, "Kenny,
what good do you think this will do? They'll only take
you back to the hospital." Then it was there interposed
a fit and he dropped the dog beside the well and fell
to the ground and cut himself with the flailing blade.
I stepped on the hand that held the knife and watched
him twist like a snake with its neck pinned down.
He frothed at the mouth and swallowed his tongue.
I tried to stick my finger in and pull it out
but he clenched his teeth in a human vise.
I thought in retrospect I could have cut a hole
in his throat with the knife but he was writhing
to the end, turning blue. I watched his ghost
shut down his skin, then disappear inside the well.
I held his body as a souvenir of the fallen world

and thought no less of him. The little dog began to bark
from the edge of the woods. "Shut up!" I yelled.
"Shut up!" and almost felt what Kenny felt as he held
the dog above the well and dangled it like the angry god
who'd crossed a wire inside his head. It was his hatred
for the little dog that had set him off, just its yapping
every night in Mrs. Smith's adjacent room. He had been
treated kindly by everyone, according to the wishes
of our saintly mother, Dorothy Day, who had always said,
"Treat every stranger as if he were the Christ."

INSIDE THE FIRE

You see that everyone is famous.
You hardly know what to say.
"It is a great honor to meet you."
"I am fortunate indeed to make your acquaintance."
But who wouldn't think you were being facetious?
You see with the sight of burning eyes.
The faces inside the faces.
They are the children of fire with classic features,
no matter who they are, no matter how deformed.
They are the stars in the only theater,
each brilliant actor in the role of her life.
Each face burns with a different light.
Blow on the soul.
See the face.
Blow on the soul.
See the face.
Look away.

THE DIN OF RINGERS

The din of ringers chimes the park
on playoff night. They come like pilgrims
from across the earth to pitch
their shoes in waking sleep. They dream
of lofting them from the driven stakes
beneath the lights. A man from Keene
has won and lost for half a century,
and now he feels the right to boast.

These masters aren't themselves
but someone else they call themselves.
Possessed with play, they walk like souls
and swing their arms. They weigh the earth
on letting go: "Forget the horse
and find the center." The earth is warm
and horses wild for a single night
in mid-September. You hear this clank
of steel on steel from over there
without regard for time or sleep
and think a man is mad somewhere
the way he strikes with futile force.

HOUSES

How many houses must one man build
before he's granted the gift of tongues?
What is the same—this beatless pounding
throughout the day, this Latin text too long
for the world—contains the future core,
a chemical built for days, at least for a while.
How else to explain the happy man
beneath the floor, without a light, who says,
"This is the day the Lord hath made."
Who finds the language within the language
to make a joke about the post that isn't plumb
and the sawyer's blade, for whom the sound
of plank on plank establishes the right palaver.
I watch the world create itself, evolve
of its own accord and am not convinced
of a worthy house. I leave a note inside
the walls of every job: *Foxes have their holes . . .*
Kindness lives from hand to mouth.
It is my life, conceding to build what cannot stand.
I feel like a ghost inside my shirt.
This is the bonus of a man at work.
My hammer is ready before the nail.

TIME WAS

this winding outside
of infinite clocks, katydids,
and no sound of ticking.
One good shot down the line
alters my view of the entire game.
I laugh at my woods, then double-fault.

Time was
a television set
above the trees beyond the courts:
a show of clocks that flickered
on and off with false alarms.
I saw it in my sleep.
Can I believe without a sign?
Not if I must ask.

Time was
the win that causes a stir
and sudden embrace of things
as they are. What did you say
in the wake of applause?
"I do not wish to prove
that anything exists per se,
only that some existing thing
is a katydid, tooth, or song."

Time was
I hardly thought of form
but simply hit.

THE DOLPHIN

My dearest parents, what did you expect?
That paradise was a place
where I could live and reign?
I'll try to explain.

I was blind with seeing inside the walls
where beauty starves on beauty.
I'm on the verge of speaking things
I can not know without the stones' assistance.
Those men, for instance, without their teeth,
the corpse I saw beside the river, inspired me
to search the earth piece by piece
until I learned that the air breathed me
when I ran my hand through the dead man's hair.

I was extinguished in the pleasance of sala trees.
A fire blazed inside my head like a flower.
I saw two things as one and multiplied the rest.
It never ends, this carrying over of other things,
this chorus of voices inside the river.

I read the sky "like a book on rising."
It said, "Difference is the soul of fire."
It said, "You are beyond me."
A caveat of clouds admonished me:
"When there is no wind lids descend as open eyes.
The worm expires inside the body."

One stone cried out beside another,
"Your body is the discipline of your desire
to turn into ten thousand things."
I believe that this is true.
How else to explain my love for the world,

my need to dance from here to there,
my need to sit beneath this tree?

Love, your son.

ALIBI

"I was waiting in the atrium of Providence Place
for my mother who was taking forever
as she always does, searching the racks
for just the right threads. I was sitting like a saint
before the era of saints as she wandered inside
for a hundred years. I was wondering after
so long a time, which is the body and which the clothes,
although I would never ask her this.
I was staring at the girls behind the window
when she emerged in a purple robe,
the same old garb in which she arrived.
I was practically grown, almost a giant
with the Nimrod nose. 'What's a mother to wear?'
she asked, 'at the end of the world?'
It was raining like never before.
We were in it, Lord, the whole blessed time.
How did she look as she went under?
Where were you when I called your name?"

THE PRESENT

lies between our breathing in and out,
like a face.
   The future is a lake or river for now,
something I can float on to the hidden shore,
something I can imagine as already true
but has yet to burn in the house of experience
that isn't consumed.
      If the lake were drained
or the river low in the season of rain, then
the flames would diminish and char the house.
The house would construct itself with flames.

The present is the past already when the flames
are gone and the roof has fallen through
the upper stories, and the owners dream but wake
too slow.
   The present is the past already when
we can see our hands like leaves in the sky.
I'm flying from Nineveh to Atlantic City but am not
inspired by where I've been.
         I've seen the children's
dress of wilted flowers on the decks of passing ships
and heard the talk across the waves day and night
on how the human race says when.

THE THIN TIME

It was the thin time when grass turns brown
and ghosts rise up to join the clouds.

You lay like an argument against the sky
and listened to the flies' diminuendo.

Oh, how they soloed in the cool October air!
Oh, how they testified against the plaster!

A door closed gently down the hall
and the furnace blew a blast of air.

You turned to the light on the distant hills.
How like a page from heaven it fell

into the oven of darkness. "What an oven
of darkness am I," you buzzed to the flies above.

The flies, the light, the closing door—
so much news to tell that can't be told.

Who to tell and how to tell it? The stars
were singing and the darkness blooming.

My deep deaf ear lay ringing beside you.
There was no speech then or now, nor were there words.

THE LAST JUDGMENT

The bodies are gorgeous in their deposition,
mesomorphs in a futile struggle to gain
the holy atom that raised the martyrs up.
Demons glom onto their thighs
with the grip of a lion on a slow gazelle.

They plummet in the nude with the terrible knowledge
that they were wicked beyond the pale.
Unrepentant.
Really bad.

St. Bartholomew's skin hangs
from his grip like a souvenir.
He's double now that he's *here*.
A joke redeems the scene: the artist's face appears
in place of the tortured saint's.
Self-portrait as signature.
This small relief.

THE CRIPPLING FIELD

You can hardly walk or run across it
without turning your ankle, without cursing it
and Fred Knapp too, without seeing it
in your mind as a harrowed field rife with wheat—
perfect for falling to your knees for a minute,
perfect for feeling level and one with it.
But no, not since Fred saw fit
in the summer of 1970 to let
the field go fallow, to sow his grief in it,
so all the childless years he tended it
were turned under and left the day she quit.
His echo still sounds *The hell with it*
from off the roofless barn where the tractor sits
unused, the plow still hitched to it.

HAROLD BLOOM

Too conscious of our need for pillows,
he rises from bed to walk the streets.
No need he thinks for underwear or other gauze
to dress his soul. Because he is alone

This late at night we can forgive
his need for walking out beyond his robe.
He is that near to seeing himself
as a sleeping coil on a marble step,

skein of flesh as subterfuge from head to toe,
that all the night becomes his clothes.
The light of day will clear his head
of false details, or he will fail to make it home.

I STAND BENEATH THE MOUNTAIN
WITH AN ILLITERATE HEART

I stand beneath the mountain with an illiterate heart
and grieve the disappearance of frogs.
How many cycles of moonless nights must I endure
before I see the grass anew and hear the song
of its growing, and know, as I did last night
in the early dark, that it is beautiful
for reasons I don't understand?

I stand beneath the mountain with an illiterate heart
and know there is a force beyond imagination
whose mercy is that it shows no mercy
with a blindness proportionate to ours.
Call it the overimagination or flower.
It hovers above the mind with wings, deferential wings,
philosophical wings, invisible wings,
and keeps us taut between earth and sky.

I stand beneath the mountain with an illiterate heart
and know that energy formed as a particle somewhere
and grew in size until it reached a critical mass
and blew apart, whereby the idea for order emerged
ironically and grass arrived in boxcars on the plains
where it sat for *days* awaiting the open hand
to finish the waters.

I stand beneath the mountain with an illiterate heart
and listen to the sky's pneumonic breathing.
I cannot think and wonder simultaneously.
I cannot use the microscope in an emergency.
This is proof that days are the enemy of memory.
What I remember lives on paper awaiting fire.
I use the paper to wrap up stones as gifts for the dead.

I stand beneath the mountain with an illiterate heart
and imagine the clouds as angels.
"This term *pain*," they say in every weather,
"we do not know. Please explain. Is it like darkness
or water or the face of the deep? Is it like light
or creeping thing? You are all such experts at this charade."

I stand beneath the mountain with an illiterate heart
and watch the frogs disappear. They are being sucked out
through a hole in the sky. I am standing now on the step,
waiting to go. A year is a day. The reel-to-reel is wailing.
"No," I say. "Yes. I mean no!"

IN THE ETERNITY THAT
WAS A DAY

In the eternity that was a day
I lay in my hammock reading
Cervantes from morning to night.
There I hung between earth and sky,
reading, reading, then stopping
for a while to contemplate the errant
knight, to weigh and consider
his madness on the plain, to ride
with him and Sancho Panza to the end.
I thought as I read that eternity
was put in my mind as a consolation.
How else could I also listen
to the birds in the maples as I read?
How else could I also smell the lilacs
in the breeze as I thought?
Never mind not knowing what God
has done from beginning to end.
When the sun went down, I slept
with the book still open across my head.
The stars broke out and the moon
rose up like Dulcinea. It was
a day that did not end and did.
That held its lamp in the dark
for me to read and think, think
and read, if only for a moment.

OUR EYES ARE SWEET,
OBEDIENT DOGS

The mind must reach beyond time,
not revise or think at all.
Thought is always late for truth.
Take the one bright element
from heaven on earth, the blazing
word inside the throats of rivers
and sky, deserts and fields,
that will not burn, and speak
its flame without a sound.
Fire catches in sight and feeds
on gross imagination.
We do not see for fear of burning here alive.

TREE OF WISDOM

I am taken in by its stand and breadth,
marveling at its brawn and reach of branches,
studying each leaf like the page of a sacred book,
embracing its trunk like a void.

I hear the prophecy of a lark in the density
of foliage: "The vision awaits its time;
hastens to the end." Until this *time* arrives,
I am content to sit and stare and climb.

I am compelled to bet my life on the fact
that this is the first work of revelation,
calling a tree *tree,* leaves *leaves.*
It is the good work of a scientist.
It is the hidden work of a common man.

I say its name like the bird who can't stop singing,
Ten Thousand Things In One, and then this prayer,
Om mani padme hum. The jewel is in the world.

I lie in the shade of its canopy
and listen to the genius above deny her name.
I turn its green to black in order to turn
it back again. I watch its fruit fall in the wind
like proofs for a law that only exists in the mind.

Like a well-stocked house it sustains me,
cleans my lungs with *the distillation.*
It is my home of transformation
where I remain and disappear.

I SEE THEM NOW

the invisible bodies rising
from the ground. How slowly
they lift themselves at first
to their elbows, as if they were
still bodies, then suddenly
to their knees, faster and faster,
until they free themselves
from the earth, higher and higher,
these blessed bodies speeding
like arrows toward a hole
in the sky, which is the sky
now that they are rising,
gaining a new oblivious
knowledge as they rise
of what it means to slip away,
to be forgotten, to say
good-bye without ever saying it,
burning as they rise, hotter
and hotter, on the one drop of fuel
that stayed inside them.

ACKNOWLEDGMENTS

The author is grateful to the following magazines in which the poems from this manuscript previously appeared: *Agni* ("The Din of Ringers," "From the Beginning On"); *Agni Online* ("Inside the Fire"); *Alembic* ("Cave Text"); *American Poetry Review* ("I See Them Now," "Last Judgment"); *American Scholar* ("To Hear and Hear"); *Boulevard* ("From the Curriculum of a Guilty Man"); *Crazyhorse* ("The Metaphysics of Husbandry," "The Sting"); *ForPoetry* ("Dinner with Charlie"); *Gettysburg Review* ("In the Eternity That Was a Day," "An Incident at the Catholic Worker," "Raiding the Bees"); *Greensboro Review* ("Anniversary"); *Iowa Review* ("The Dolphin," "The Field," under the title "Two Fields"); *Marlboro Review* ("The Overstory"); *Natural Bridge* ("Kitty"); *New England Review* ("The Fox," "Houses," "Night Mowing," "The Present"); *New Republic* ("Yellow Jackets"); *North American Review* ("Shaman"); *North Dakota Quarterly* ("Catch," "The Crippling Field," "Sighting," "Whales"); *Ploughshares* ("Alibi," "Harold Bloom," "Sugaring"); *Poetry East* "The Birds," "Hammock," "Our Eyes Are Sweet, Obedient Dogs"); *Prose Poem* ("The Music"); *Quarterly West* ("Time Was"); *Seneca Review* ("Sleeping Lessons"); *Smartish Pace* ("December 10," "Frog"); *Sonora Review* ("Margaret Miller's Arm"); *Southern Review* ("A Day in the Life," "Field Work," under the title "Good Dog"); *Texas Review* ("Gatsby Presents His Case to the Sport of Heaven"); *Witness* ("First Touch," "I Get Up When I'm Dead," "Through a Train Window"); *Worcester Review* ("The Thin Time").

"I Stand Beneath the Mountain with an Illiterate Heart" appeared in *Poems for a Small Planet: Contemporary American Nature Poetry* (1993).

"The Music" appeared in *Best of the Prose Poem: An International Journal* (2000).

I would like to thank the following people for their invaluable editorial, critical, and emotional help in the making of this book: Bruce Smith, Jacqueline Gens, Jerry Stern, Ed Ochester, Deborah Meade, Peter Johnson, Brian Cohen, Jane Lunin Perel, Jeff Friedman, Stephen Sandy, and David Calicchio.